The
Adventures
of
Francelia
Whitefoot

by

John Higby

**Illustrations
by
Warren Dennis**

1999

**Parkway Publishers, Inc.
Boone, North Carolina**

Available from:

Parkway Publishers, Inc.
P. O. Box 3678
Boone, North Carolina 28607
Telephone/Facsimile: (828) 265-3993

Library of Congress Cataloging-in-Publication Data

Higby, John. 1936–
    Francelia / by John Higby : illustrations by Warren Dennis.
        p. cm.
    Summary: Having been abandoned by her sophisticated but
shallow husband, Francelia the mouse is left to raise her fourteen
children with the help of the other animals in Sweetgrass Meadow.
    ISBN: 1-887905-16-2
    [1. Mice Fiction. 2. Animals Fiction.] I. Dennis, Warren, 1927–
ill. II. Title.
PZ7.H5344Fr 1999
[Fic]--dc21
                                                                    99-25134
                                                                        CIP

It was generally agreed by those who knew her that Francelia Whitefoot was the loveliest creature in all of Sweetgrass Meadow. How the beauty of a mouse can be compared to that of a bluebird, a toad, a swallow, or a garter snake is admittedly hard to determine, but Francelia's eyes were so dark and shining, her whiskers so neatly groomed, her fur so rich and lustrous, and her figure and tiny claws so delicately shaped that no one believed it possible anything or anyone could be more handsome. In addition, Francelia had perfectly huge ears and an extraordinarily long tail, the two things a mouse must have if she is to be more than merely pretty.

Francelia lived with her parents in a nest of soft grasses, hidden in the roots of a great oak tree that stood near one corner of the meadow. All of her many brothers and sisters had moved away to their own places, but she chose to remain at home, where she led a very comfortable life. Her father had grown rich through his association with mice who lived in the dairy barn across the meadow. Long ago he had arranged to buy cheese from the barn mice, which he then sold at a profit not only to his mouse neighbors but several families of chipmunks and an occasional rat who was passing through. The best pieces of cheese he kept for his own use, so that Francelia and her mother were very well fed. To keep from growing fat, they played endless games of tag and hide-and-seek around the roots of the great oak tree and in a tangle of blackberry bushes that grew beside it. In season they would gather berries to follow the cheese course at dinner. When they were tired from games or berrying, they would sun themselves on a bare rock, always keeping close to shelter, out of danger from hawks that occasionally flew over the field. Neither Francelia nor her parents ever went out at night, for everybody knew that the owls who lived in the woods at the far end of the meadow appeared as soon as the sun went down. Their frightful cries could be heard as they flew about looking for a quick and easy meal.

One day the barn mice came for a visit, partly to conduct business with Francelia's father and partly for the pleasure of a picnic out of doors. They brought with them a large piece of a delicious new cheese, which had become available through the skill of a man who had begun working in the dairy. Of course Francelia and her parents were invited to taste this delicacy, which went especially well with the blackberries that had just come into season. After dinner Francelia's father and the barn mice went for a stroll in the meadow, and when they returned, Francelia and her mother could see that they were all talking very earnestly. Francelia's mother grew worried, for her father was not an excitable man, and something extraordinary had to be taking place for him to be so aroused. But when the barn mice prepared to leave, there were smiles and shaking of paws all around, which tended to restore calm in the nest.

That night Francelia, who had gone to bed early, heard her father talking to her mother about the wonderful life of the mice in the dairy barn. They had worlds of cheese and milk if they wished it. The barn was always warm and snug in bad weather. There were endless dark corners and high shelves for playing mouse games, marvelous bright machines that made a great spectacle for the curious, and no danger at all from hawks and owls.

"What about cats?" asked Francelia's mother. "Surely there must be a cat, or maybe even many cats."

Well, yes, there *was* a cat, admitted Francelia's father,

but he was a great, fat, lazy tom who had his own basket in the milk room and a huge saucer of cream at breakfast and at suppertime. No one could remember when the cat last chased a mouse; he was not even regarded as an enemy by the barn mice. Francelia's father could say nothing but good about the dairy barn and the lives of the mice who lived there. He concluded by announcing that he thought the Whitefoots ought to move to the barn themselves.

"I've worked hard," he said, "and now I want to enjoy life. If we move to the barn we'll never need to worry again. We'll have a snug home and lots of interesting things to do. The biggest danger will be from a cat that's too well-fed and too lazy to chase even goldfish pulling a wagonload of catnip." He went on to say that he had already begun to plan for the move, knew an enterprising young mouse to take over his cheese business, and required only that Francelia's mother agree to his proposal. They could be resettled in three days.

"For myself," said Francelia's mother, "I could find living in the barn very pleasant. There would be more fine company to be sure, and I always have been one to appreciate the advantages of a civilized environment. I am positively tired of the lack of refinement one sometimes encounters here in the meadow. I don't think, however, that the barn would be good for Francelia. After all, she is of an age to think of a home and family of her own, and I don't approve of the eligible mice in the barn. They are dull-witted and fat from over-eating, and they give themselves airs.

4

Besides, most of them pick up shreds of tobacco that fall from the pockets of the men in the barn and chew it. No daughter of mine is going to build a nest and begin a family with an overweight mouse who chews tobacco. The very thought of it makes me shudder. My great-aunt had a tobacco chewer for a mate and he gave her nothing but grief. When I think of the trouble that she went through because of tobacco it makes me. . .."

Francelia heard her father interrupt in soothing tones intended to calm her mother's agitation. He assured Francelia's mother that he would do nothing hasty, that they would consider Francelia's future carefully, and that there was no need to get excited at bedtime and suffer all night from indigestion. Furthermore, he said, everything would appear in a different light after a good night's sleep. He quite agreed that Francelia should be kept away from bad influences, but felt quite sure something satisfactory could be worked out.

"Well, I suppose you're right," said Francelia's mother, growing calmer. "I would like the barn life very well, you see, but I'm sure it's all wrong for Francelia. We must consider her too. But tomorrow is soon enough to find a solution to our problem. After all, tomorrow is another day."

Chapter Two

In spite of the furor that Francelia had overheard the night before, she slept soundly and awoke early before her parents were stirring. It was a fine summer's day, and she decided to have a walk in the meadow to whet her appetite for breakfast cheese. Sweetgrass Meadow was alive with her friends and acquaintances — bluebirds, larks, swallows, a toad or two, and a whole family of garter snakes slithering about in the rich grass from which the dew was quickly drying. She stopped to chat with one or two of her chipmunk friends, and even exchanged a courteous greeting with a great bullfrog sunning himself by the edge of the small pond. There were no hawks in the sky; the owls had long since returned to the woods to sleep through the day. Everywhere she looked Francelia saw creatures for whom she felt affection, and it came to her that whatever her parents chose to do, she could not be happy living away from the meadow and its pleasures. She was not troubled by this thought, but rather realized as she walked about that she was, after all, a nearly adult mouse who should be able to decide her own future.

When she returned home, Francelia found her parents at breakfast. She saw as she joined them that nothing had been settled. Strangely quiet, they seemed to find it difficult to speak to Francelia or even to look at her. Francelia decided that it would be best if she spoke first. When breakfast was finished, she began:

"I must confess," she said, "that I overheard you talking after I went to bed last night, and I understand why you find it difficult to talk to me this morning. I don't want you uncomfortable on my account," she continued, "and there is no reason why you should be. Life in the barn would be wonderful for you, and I think you should move there if you want. I don't want to move from Sweetgrass Meadow. All my friends are here, and those fancy, tobacco-chewing young mice in the barn don't interest me in the least. I am practically grown up now and feel sure I can look after myself. I have this cozy nest to live in, and though I might find it pleasant to have a mate and a family, I am in no hurry. I am sure a nice young mouse with good prospects will turn up someday, and until that happens, I am content to wait and be happy with my friends. Please, go ahead with your plans and don't worry about me."

All of this sounded very sensible to Francelia's parents, although her mother continued to fret for most of the morning. She imagined all kinds of trouble that Francelia might face in the absence of her parents' guidance, and for each difficulty that she imagined, a reassuring solution had to be found.

It was decided that the move to the barn would not take place for three more days. Everyone would have a chance to adjust to the new arrangements and for it to become known that Francelia would be living alone. Her parents felt that if all Francelia's friends among the meadow creatures knew that she was by herself — and probably a little lonely at first — they would pitch in as good neighbors always do and help her adjust to her new situation. Francelia's father would have a chance to hand over his cheese business, and time to locate a comfortable nook in the dairy barn for himself and Francelia's mother.

The next three days were very busy ones. As Francelia's father tidied up his affairs, her mother scurried about the meadow informing her neighbors that they were leaving, extracting promises that Francelia would be looked after and kept from unsettling difficulties. Through all of this Francelia remained serene, confident that she would get along very nicely. She was proud to think that she would now be regarded as a fully adult mouse, mistress of her own affairs. She noticed that several of the eligible young mice in the meadow spent more time than usual around her nest during these days, as if offering to become her protectors after her parents had gone, but none of them seemed particularly handsome or clever to her. Though she was polite to them all, she did nothing to offer any of them any encouragement.

When her parents' moving day arrived, Francelia got up early and put out an especially tasty piece of cheese for their breakfast. Her father ate heartily, but her mother was upset and tearful and could only nibble. By midmorning everything was in order. Francelia's father, though clearly he would miss his daughter, was excited about the new life he was beginning and eager to be on his way.

Francelia's mother was clearly upset and full of concerns about her daughter's well-being. "Remember the owls and promise me you'll never go out at night, Francelia. Stay away from the pond, Francelia – you know you're not a strong swimmer. Be sure to add more grass to the nest before cold weather comes. Keep the cheese in a cool spot where it won't spoil. Promise me you won't go out with any roughneck mice or get involved with anyone who chews tobacco." To all these warnings Francelia offered a sweet smile and the correct response. At last her mother was satisfied that all would be well, and with a final exchange of embraces and promises to send news back and forth between the meadow and the barn, the elder Whitefoots departed.

Nothing remarkable happened in the first days of Francelia's independence. She was visited frequently by her friends. A family of chipmunks brought her a parcel of especially tasty seeds they had gathered. Two or three eligible young mice invited her to small games of hide-and-seek. One evening a whole choir of swallows came to serenade her. None of the quiet pleasures with which she filled her time prepared her for the remarkable event that was soon to come to pass.

Chapter Three

One day, about a week after Francelia's parents moved away, a great, long, shining automobile came down the dirt road that stopped at the edge of the meadow. The people who alighted from it were far more richly dressed than the men in the dairy barn, and their speech did not sound the same.

It soon became obvious that they had arrived for a picnic, and no ordinary picnic at that! A fine white cloth was spread on the ground, and large hampers of food and bottles with long green necks were placed about it. All of the meadow creatures gathered to watch the proceedings from convenient places of shelter, their mouths watering as they contemplated the many delicious bits of fruit and crumbs of cake that would be left behind.

Francelia curiously watched a young boy who had come with the party. He carried a small, gilded cage which seemed to contain a pet of some sort. After the picnic had well begun, the boy opened the door of the cage and let his pet out to run about, but Francelia was not close enough to see clearly what manner of creature it was. The picnic lasted so long that all of Francelia's friends finally grew impatient for the people to be gone.

"What's taking them so long?" grumbled a chipmunk. "I have an appointment to keep, and if they don't leave soon, I won't be here to share in the feast."

"If they don't leave soon," complained a toad, "ants will have already carried away all the best crumbs."

Finally the picnic appeared to be drawing to a close. A commotion developed when the boy's pet couldn't be found, though everyone searched industriously. Finally the man in charge began speaking sharply, pointing to the watch on his wrist and explaining to the sobbing boy that there was nothing more to be done. The car was loaded and the people drove away, taking with them the boy for whom the outing had ended as a very sad affair.

Quickly the meadow creatures moved to the site of the picnic, and indeed the litter the people had left behind was all they could have hoped for. There were bits of fruit and cheese, a crust of bread, cake crumbs, and several cookies

that had not even been broken. Francelia, always careful not to eat too much and more dainty than many of her neighbors, kept at the edge of the party. After finding one or two cake crumbs that particularly suited her, she said farewell to her friends and started toward her nest at the base of the great oak tree.

It was growing dark, and Francelia decided to take a short cut through a large clump of especially thick grass that stood between her and the oak tree. A path hidden in this grass had been built by her father as a refuge for anyone caught away from home when the hawks came over the meadow. She had proceeded down this path but a little way when she was suddenly confronted with the greatest surprise she had experienced in her short life.

There before her was a perfectly white mouse. He had a marvelous pink nose, simply enormous ears, and an acceptably long tail. Francelia knew immediately that this was the boy's lost pet, for around his neck was tied a bit of dark blue silk ribbon with tiny silver polka dots. Francelia thought he was the finest, handsomest mouse she had ever seen, and she suddenly grew shy. But the mouse struck up a conversation as if he had expected Francelia to come down this path and already knew what he was going to say.

"Well good afternoon, Pretty Miss. My name is Alfonzo, but I can see immediately that I shall want you to call me Alfie. I don't allow many creatures that liberty, but for you I shall certainly make an exception."

Francelia felt very confused and completely incapable of replying to this handsome young mouse. She felt herself blushing and hoped that the color wouldn't show through her thick, glossy fur.

"I say," continued Alfonzo, "I seem to be in a bit of a pickle. I decided this afternoon that I wanted to be done with my cage and the people who have been keeping me and ran away, but now I find that I don't very well know how to manage my new freedom. I have no place to sleep tonight, no food, and no clear idea of the dangers to be avoided in this lovely meadow. Angelic as you appear, perhaps you will consent to be my guardian and help me through my first difficulties. I promise that I shall be most

attentive to your instruction. It will be my singular good luck to have so charming a guide as I embark on my new adventures." Concluding, Alfonzo smiled at Francelia so charmingly that she felt her face turn utterly scarlet, but he appeared to notice nothing unusual and went on.

"Be so kind as to let me attend you home," he said. "You can point out things of interest along the way and perhaps introduce some of your friends to me. I'll also need to find a safe place to sleep tonight. I won't need anything to eat, for I had all I could possibly eat at the picnic. Please answer me now. I feel sure that your voice matches your splendid person, and I shall not be content until I have heard it."

Francelia attempted a reply and was horrified to discover that she could do little more than squeak. "Welcome — *squeak* — to our meadow, Alfonzo -- *squeak*. I am sure — *squeak, squeak* — you will find this — *squeak* — a very pleasant place to live — *squeak* — but you must — *squeak* — be very careful until you understand — *squeak* — the dangers here. Your white coat — *squeak* — would be a very easy thing for the hawks or owls to see — *squeak, squeak*."

Alfonzo seemed not to notice the squeaking. "I shall be careful," he said, "but if you will permit me a little boasting, I am a very clever mouse. I have had to be to deal with the boy who kept me. But you haven't said you will let me walk you home. Please say that you'll give me that happiness. And please call me just Alfie."

"If you would like to walk me home, I would be happy to have your company," said Francelia, blushing again, but at least not squeaking. "We must go quickly, though, as it is almost dusk and we must be safely hidden away before then." With that she turned toward her nest. Alfonzo ran to catch up, and Francelia also began to run, so that they both arrived at the base of the great oak tree laughing and breathless.

"Here is where I live," said Francelia, shyly. "There is an old chipmunk den under a root on the other side of the tree. You can sleep there tonight and then tomorrow I will help you find something better."

Alfonzo stood on his hind legs and made Francelia a deep, gentlemanly bow. "For your kind attention, Pretty Miss, I am altogether grateful. I shall sleep more soundly because I have such delightful prospects for the morrow. And now I suppose I must bid you good night."

"Good night," she said. "And by the way, my name is Francelia."

"Good night, Francelia," he said, and again he gave her his charming smile.

Chapter Four

Francelia slept late the next morning, so that when she emerged from her nest the next morning, the sun was high in the sky. Just outside her door she found a bouquet of bright blue cornflowers, which seemed almost certainly a gift from Alfonzo. None of the young mice in the meadow had ever thought to bring her flowers. Francelia went to the chipmunk den on the other side of the oak tree, expecting to find her new friend near his quarters, but Alfonzo was nowhere to be seen.

She found him part way down a broad path, seemingly surrounded by half the creatures of Sweetgrass Meadow, whom he had captivated in a twinkling with stories of his wonderful adventures as the pet of a wealthy boy. Standing quietly at the edge of the crowd, Francelia heard Alfonzo tell of visiting Europe in a jet plane, of sailing in a swift boat off the Atlantic Coast, of watching mouse stories on television, of sleeping in a nest of silk and woolen scraps. He described the pleasures of ice cream, milk chocolate, peanuts, and popcorn. He had seen a baseball game, a tennis match, a horse race, and a golf course. He had ridden an elevator to the top of a skyscraper. There seemed to be nothing that he hadn't done and nowhere that he hadn't been.

Francelia could see that Alfonzo was going to get on very well with the meadow creatures — all, that is, but a few of the young mice, who were clearly a little jealous of this worldly young adventurer. Even they grew more friendly, however, when Alfonzo began to describe the games he knew how to play. He knew several varieties of tag and hide-and-seek, knew how to organize country dances in which nearly all the creatures of the meadow could participate, and even proposed how they might construct a gymnasium for the pleasure of all except possibly the toads and frogs, whom he remembered by suggesting the establishment of a leaping and swimming society.

Suddenly Alfonzo spied Francelia at the edge of the gathering and caused her great embarrassment by giving up his fascinating talk to come quickly to her side.

"Good morning, my dear Francelia," he said. "I trust you have slept well. I thought it better not to disturb you this morning, and as you can see, I have undertaken to become acquainted with your delightful neighbors."

"Good morning, Alfonzo," said Francelia. "Thank you for the lovely flowers."

"Did you like them?" he asked. "Then the trouble of gathering them has been my day's first happiness." Speaking more quietly he said, "Alfie, Alfie. The others shall call me Alfonzo, but you alone must call me Alfie."

Francelia blushed scarlet.

Alfonzo then turned back to address the others. "You must excuse us for the moment," he said. "I promised

Francelia a stroll in the meadow this morning, and now I have the good fortune to be allowed to fulfill my pledge. If you all will meet me here after lunch, I shall teach you an especially interesting form of tag that I have learned during my travels."

Francelia remembered no promise about a stroll in the meadow, but she allowed herself to be led away. She was amazed at Alfonzo's ability to talk so interestingly and with such little effort. For herself, all she could manage during their walk was to answer the questions that were directed to her. She did remember to give Alfonzo further warning about the hawks and the owls, and found that as the morning wore on, it was less difficult to speak to Alfonzo and occasionally to look into his face. Once she even managed not to blush when Alfonzo smiled at her.

Near lunchtime Francelia remembered that she had not yet eaten that day. Alfonzo had not eaten either, as it turned out, and she invited him back to her nest for some cheese newly arrived from the dairy barn. She was afraid that so fine a mouse as he would not relish ordinary cheese, but he appeared to consider her luncheon delicious. He even climbed into a blackberry bramble and fetched down several especially juicy berries for dessert.

"You know," he said as he finished his berries, "you have not yet called me Alfie. I hope you don't think me impertinent to ask that you use that name. You are, after all, my first acquaintance in the meadow, and I think our friendship should be special, with special names. Would it help if I called you Celia?" he asked. "Francelia is really too stiff and formal a name for a pretty young maiden like you."

Francelia blushed and said nothing.

"Come now, Celia. Let me hear you say 'Alfie.'"

"*Squeak* — Alfie." Francelia was furious with herself for the squeak.

"Try again, Celia."

"Alfie," she said.

"Excellent, my dear Celia," replied Alfonzo. "You did it just right." He and Francelia gathered up the luncheon things and put them away and returned to the meadow for the promised game of tag. News of Alfonzo and his clever talk and many accomplishments had spread quickly, and it seemed that nearly every friendly creature in Sweetgrass Meadow had gathered for the game. Alfonzo taught them something called Chinese tag, which required that whoever was tagged must hold the part of his body that had been touched while pursuing someone new to be "it." Everything went very well until a toad was tagged on his hind foot. Trying to chase others while holding a hind foot proved so difficult that the toad finally gave up and the game came to an end. The garter snakes then pointed out that they really had felt excluded from the game anyway, since there was no way for them to hold one part of the body with another. Alfonzo acknowledged that he had not been fully considerate of all his new neighbors and promised to do better in arranging future games.

The rest of the afternoon was uneventful. Alfonzo entertained all who remained with a full account of his airplane trip to Europe. Once hawks appeared in the sky at the far end of the meadow, causing everyone to scurry for shelter, but the danger soon passed. The brief threat of trouble seemed to spoil the mood of the day, however, and before long the gathering began to break up. Francelia invited Alfonzo to eat with her again. At dinner he seemed more quiet and serious than Francelia had yet seen him. Shortly after the meal had ended he excused himself and, bidding Francelia — or Celia, as he called her — good night, he returned to the chipmunk den to sleep.

Chapter Five

The next morning Francelia awoke to find another bouquet of cornflowers at her front door. This time there was also a basket of fruit in the form of several large, sweet blackberries placed in a large empty nutshell. Alfonzo had already departed the chipmunk den, so Francelia was unable to thank him for his gifts right away. She encountered him about an hour later at the edge of the pond, where he was engaged in helping the frogs and toads draw up a charter for their leaping and swimming society. Upon Francelia's appearance he concluded his business rapidly and excused himself to walk with her in the meadow as he had done the day before.

After lunch Alfonzo organized a country dance for all the meadow creatures, which was even better received than the Chinese tag game. He even persuaded an assortment of the songbirds and several crickets, who normally refrain from chirruping until evening, to provide music for the affair. Alfonzo dined with Francelia at dusk, but this night he seemed in no hurry to leave, and visited with Francelia until a rather late hour. He continued to fascinate her with stories of marvelous things he had seen and done, but he seemed increasingly careful not to sound boastful and encouraged Francelia to talk about herself. She was still confused and somewhat embarrassed by his charming smile and phrases such as "dear Celia" and "pretty miss," but found that she was growing to like them.

When Alfonzo finally bid her good night and returned to the chipmunk den to sleep, she found herself worrying about the small danger in scurrying to the other side of the great oak tree at night. She wasn't entirely relieved until she saw him the next morning.

The activities of Alfonzo's first days in the meadow seemed to establish a pattern. Each morning Francelia would find flowers or other gifts at her door, and find Alfonzo engaged in a project with some of her neighbors when she went into the meadow. This would be followed by their stroll, lunch, games in the meadow, dinner, quiet conversation, and finally a parting between Francelia and Alfonzo when it was time for him to return to the chipmunk den.

One afternoon when games were finished and Francelia and Alfonzo were returning to the great oak tree, a shadow passed over them and then back again. Francelia knew immediately that they were in terrible danger.

"It's the hawks, Alfie! Run, follow me quickly."

Francelia dashed for her nest. For a moment it appeared that Alfonzo would not make it, but with a final effort he raced into the safety of the nest just as a hawk swooped down to grasp him. Both Francelia and Alfonzo were so breathless that they could not speak. They huddled together and peered out of the nest, where two fierce hawks were circling. There would be no going back into the meadow that day. For the rest of the afternoon and evening she and Alfonzo huddled together in the nest with no thought of dinner or a quiet visit. They were both much too upset to enjoy such pleasures.

That night Alfonzo did not return to the chipmunk den. It may be that Francelia needed him to calm her terror — or, that Alfonzo needed her company for the same reason. In any case, Alfonzo remained with Francelia that night, and within a few days it was obvious to everyone that Alfonzo and Francelia had become mates. Though there was a certain amount of jealous grumbling among the eligible young mice, most of Francelia's friends were glad that she had a partner. On the first day when Sweetgrass Meadow seemed safe from hawks, they gave her a great wedding feast. Alfonzo, who was accustomed to festive living, particularly enjoyed this celebration. He was very attentive to his bride and even recited a poem which began "Come, my Celia, let us prove," which he claimed to have written in honor of the occasion. He told an amusing little story about a town mouse and a country mouse to entertain the assembled company and again organized a country dance, after which he called for a waltz and danced with Francelia until she was breathless.

"If only we had appropriate music, my dear, I would teach you the new dances now being done in the city," Alfonzo declared. "The people with whom I used to live often had disco parties in the basement of their home, and I assure you they were lively affairs." Francelia declared that she was perfectly satisfied with old-fashioned dancing. "We'd better stop dancing for today altogether," she pointed out, as it was nearly dusk and everyone should return quickly to their homes.

"Whatever you say, my dear," replied Alfonzo. He made a little speech to all of Francelia's friends and neighbors, thanking them for the wedding feast. He made special note of Francelia's parents, who had returned to the meadow for the celebration and were looking very well. Since moving to the barn Francelia's mother had taken to curling her whiskers, and she now carried her tail with a crook that resembled the little finger of a fine lady drinking a cup of tea. As Alfonzo led Francelia away to the nest beneath the great oak tree he began to compose a new poem, which he insisted he would call "Song: To Celia." It began:

> *Drink to me only with shine eyes,*
> *And I will pledge with mine;*
> *Or leave a kiss but in the cup,*
> *And I'll not look for wine.*

But after four lines Alfonzo seemed to have trouble deciding what should come next, and resolved to work on his new poem again after they had eaten dinner.

The days that followed were extremely happy ones for Francelia and Alfonzo. Their union seemed blessed with some of the most beautiful summer weather that anyone in the meadow could remember. There was an abundance of fresh berries and flowers and practically no threat from the hawks, who seemed to be doing their hunting elsewhere. The bright daylight hours were given to endless games and dancing and flower-gathering with other creatures of the meadow. In the evening Francelia prepared exquisite little cheese dishes while Alfonzo composed new poems to recite to her when dinner was over. Her favorite was something called *"How do I love thee? Let me count the ways,"* which Alfonzo — or Alfie, as she now called him — dashed off without apparent effort in an inspired moment.

One morning the mouse who now obtained cheese from

the dairy barn came to the entrance of the nest and asked to speak to Alfonzo. Francelia remained in the nest while her mate stepped outside to see what their caller wanted. He was gone for quite some time, and when he returned, he did not look very happy.

"What is it? What's it all about, Alfie?" asked Francelia.

"Bad news, my dear," replied Alfonzo. "The men in the barn have begun locking up their cheese. We shall probably be able to get a little food from that quarter in the future, but nowhere near what we have been accustomed to."

"Well," said Francelia, "that is disturbing news, but I think we'll manage without too much trouble. There are simply loads of berries and seeds this summer, and there will be nuts in the fall. I'm sure we can gather enough to see us through the bad weather."

"That may be true, my dear," said Alfonzo, "but you will find things much less pleasant when you don't have an abundance of cheese. A good wedge of cheese gives life its zest, and you will miss it sorely when it is no longer plentiful."

In spite of her efforts to be cheerful, Francelia seemed unable to raise Alfonzo's spirits. He grew very quiet and asked to be excused from games that day. He appeared to be thinking hard about the difficulty which they now faced, and though he vowed that he would discover a happy solution to their problem, he did not look a bit hopeful.

That afternoon he went for a walk alone in the meadow, claiming that he needed a change of air and that the bright sunshine would help his attitude. After he left the nest, neither Francelia nor any other meadow creature ever saw Alfonzo again. There was no evidence that a hawk or some other fierce creature captured Alfonzo — he simply disappeared. It was rumored that a white mouse was living in the house beside the dairy barn, but nobody ever knew for sure whether it was true, or if it was, whether the white mouse was Alfonzo.

The disappearance of Alfonzo caused general sorrow in Sweetgrass Meadow and much concern for Francelia, who had lost her mate after a very short period of happiness. Many were worried that Francelia would not recover from the shock, and her friends watched her closely in the days that followed. She was visited frequently by her neighbors, who brought her good things to eat and tried hard to think of amusing, encouraging or simply comforting things to say. Francelia, though she was deeply grieved over the loss of Alfie, smiled bravely and went on as best she could. She made herself eat nourishing things and sleep regularly and go into the meadow for exercise. She did these things because she knew that even if her mate was lost and gone forever, she would soon have all the company in the nest that she could want. She knew that she would soon have her first family of baby mice.

Chapter Six

As the time approached when Francelia would give birth to her babies, she grew very busy. She added soft grasses to her nest and constructed a stout passageway of twigs at the front door so that it would be more secure. She gathered and stored seeds and berries so that there would be plenty of food. She managed to get a small bit of cheese from the barn, which she ate so that she would be strong and healthy when her family arrived. Her friends in the meadow feared she would tire herself out by her efforts and did what they could to help. Being a very sensible mouse, Francelia accepted this help graciously.

There were a few awkward moments, when some toads brought bits of food that simply were not acceptable in a mouse diet. Another time the children in a family of garter snakes came by and offered to teach Francelia's babies how to slither after they arrived. Francelia thanked them sweetly and explained that slithering, though a very fine thing in a garter snake, was not an accomplishment for which a mouse had a very great need. Because she was such a considerate, tactful creature, she was able to refuse inappropriate gifts and assistance without hurting any feelings.

Early one afternoon, at a general gathering of Francelia's friends and neighbors, who continued to enjoy the games and dances Alfonzo had taught them, a chipmunk suddenly remarked that Francelia had not been about that day. "She was fine when I spoke to her last evening," said a meadowlark. "I hope nothing is wrong."

"By my reckoning it's about time for her babies to arrive," said a wise old mouse who had brought up many children. "Perhaps someone should go and see whether she is all right."

"I can find out most quickly," said a bluebird. "I'll go and fly right back with any news I can discover. We don't want to disturb her with a lot of noisy company."

The bluebird flew away to Francelia's nest, but she didn't return very quickly. In fact, she was gone so long that the others began to worry, and there was a growing feeling that someone else should go and check on Francelia's well-being. Just then the bluebird returned, so excited that she couldn't speak at first. She did manage to nod "yes" when asked whether Francelia was all right, and she nodded "yes" again when asked whether the babies had come. Finally she grew calm enough to speak.

"Fourteen!" was all she could say at first.

"Fourteen?" chorused the meadow creatures.

"That's right. Fourteen. Francelia has fourteen tiny mice in her nest. Seven boys and seven girls." Nobody had ever heard of such a huge family. The news was simply astounding. The bluebird assured everyone that Francelia and all her babies were fine and healthy, but the new mother was tired.

"She thinks that by next week her friends can come to see her and her new family," said the bluebird, "but for the moment she is very busy. She says everything is well and she has plenty to eat, and she sends you all greetings and thanks for the help you have given her."

"Hurrah for Francelia," cried a frog.

"Hurrah for Francelia," everybody answered.

Francelia's friends were very eager to see her new family, but would not disturb her until they knew that she was ready to receive company. Finally, one morning Francelia sent word that she was prepared to see her friends and would have her family ready for display at noon.

At the appointed hour everyone who was not terribly busy moved toward the great oak tree. When the gathering seemed complete, one of the older mice went to the door of Francelia's nest and called to her. In a moment Francelia appeared at her door, and a great cheer went up from her friends. Francelia returned a pretty smile and then turned to call her family outside.

No one was quite prepared for the spectacle that Francelia now offered to the meadow creatures. Baby mice simply poured from the door of her nest. First came her seven little boys and then seven little girls, who like their mother were dainty, shy little things. How beautiful they all were! One little boy had the coat of his mother except for his head and neck, which seemed covered with a snow white hood. A sister matched him, except that the colors were reversed, so that her perfectly white body was set off with a head and neck of rich brown fur. There were two mice, a boy and a girl, who were a gorgeous silvery tan color from head to foot.

The remaining ten children were colored like painted ponies, having large patches of brown fur contrasting with similar patches of white. The little boys were already a rough-and-tumble set, full of energy and mischief. The girls were quiet and well-behaved and stayed close to their mother.

"What have you named them, Francelia?" called one of her friends.

Francelia replied that naming so many children had been a problem. She had finally decided that since their father had been such a fine gentleman, the boys should be given gentlemanly names. The white-hooded boy she had named Reginald, and the silver-tan one was Launcelot. The other boys she had named Algernon, Chauncey, Cedric, Christopher, and Sebastian. The girls were named for flowers. The dark-hooded girl was named Rose, and the silvery-tan one was Violet. The other girls were Daisy, Pansy, Lily, Tulip, and Iris. Everyone thought the names were lovely except a bullfrog named Cornelius, who grumbled that he thought Cornelius was a much finer, more gentlemanly name than Chauncey or Cedric. It was remarked that all of the little mice had their mother's large ears and long, slender tail, and it appeared that once they grew up, their whiskers would be everything a truly handsome mouse could wish for.

After everyone had gotten a thorough look at Francelia's fourteen offspring, she called her children back into the nest. They were, after all, tiny creatures still, and like all wise mothers, Francelia felt it very important that they not miss their afternoon nap. Once she saw her babies safely into shelter, she returned outside to talk with her friends for a little while.

Francelia assured everyone that although her stores were beginning to run low, she still had sufficient food for her family and was otherwise managing very nicely. She told the frog and mouse and snake and songbird children that in another week or two her babies would be able to start playing in some of the less strenuous games. Francelia recognized that summer would soon draw to a close, but she felt that with a little luck she could get her children through their early childhood before the weather began to grow harsh. It seemed to everyone that Francelia was doing well with her large family even if she had no mate to help her, and when the meadow creatures returned to their homes later that afternoon, they were all satisfied that she had her affairs very much in hand.

Chapter Seven

In the weeks that followed, Francelia's family grew into strong, healthy young mice. It was a large task to keep them all well fed and neatly groomed, but the neighbors helped as they could, and as late summer became early fall, there was an abundance of seeds from the meadow plants and apples that fell from the trees in the orchard nearby. Francelia's parents brought a gift of cheese from the barn, where they seemed fairly content even though cheese and other good things to eat were less easy to come by than they once had been. They reported that the cat at least had all the cream it wanted and continued to have no interest in chasing mice.

When they grew big enough, Francelia let her children go into the meadow to play with their friends. Because they were so brightly colored and easy to see, they had to be especially careful about the hawks, and they experienced difficulties playing hide-and-seek because their coats were so vivid. But they were excellent at tag and learned to dance so quickly that they won the prize in a square dancing contest that was held at the suggestion of a toad who fancied that no one could dance so well as he and his group. Francelia sometimes found it tiring to try to keep seven energetic little boys from playing too hard or straying too far from the nest and was grateful that her girls were such sweet, well-behaved children.

In early fall — it was about the beginning of October — Francelia had to admit to herself that she faced a serious problem. Though there were many good things to eat lying about the meadow and apples and nuts nearby, her many children had such good appetites that it was difficult to keep them all fed. She realized further that it was now necessary to build up stores that could be drawn upon when bad weather came and food was scarce. Fortunately the winters were not really harsh in Sweetgrass Meadow, and by winter her children would be old enough to help gather their own food.

Francelia was uneasy over the effort that was now required simply to see that everyone went to bed with a full stomach. She didn't want to tell her friends about her worries because she felt that they all had done quite enough to help her. Some evenings she remained in the meadow gathering food so late that she could hear the first horrible cries of the owls as they awakened from their day's sleep in the woods and began to move toward their hunting grounds.

One morning a chipmunk who passed close to the great oak tree on his way through the meadow heard unhappy squeaking coming from Francelia's nest. He scurried over to the nest and peered inside. There he found fourteen little mice all hungry and squeaking for their breakfast, but Francelia was nowhere to be seen.

He waited for a few minutes, thinking that she would soon appear with breakfast for her children. When she did not, he grew worried and went into the meadow to give the alarm that Francelia was missing.

The meadow creatures quickly organized into two groups. Half of them got breakfast for the hungry little mice while the other half searched the meadow for Francelia.

Providing breakfast was not too difficult a matter, but those who went in search of Francelia returned with the unhappy news that she was not to be found. "What a frightful situation," said the bullfrog Cornelius, in his usual grumpy manner, hiding the fact that he was really a rather good fellow.

"I hope nothing has happened to her," said a garter snake, giving a little shudder as he thought of the terrible owls.

Nothing REALLY bad could have happened to Francelia, the meadow creatures concluded. When something terrible happens, the creatures of the meadow somehow KNEW. There is no way to explain it. Since nobody had this dreadful feeling, they reasoned that Francelia, though she was missing, was probably all right, but that did not lessen the difficulty of providing for fourteen hungry little mice.

"We must look after Francelia's children until she returns," said a swallow. "It's the only civilized, neighborly thing to do."

"But we don't know how long that will be," worried a chipmunk. "My uncle once became lost while looking for nuts in the woods, and he didn't get home for eleven weeks."

"Much as I hate to say this, I think we are going to have to split the family up," said a bluebird. "Fourteen children are a great many, but if seven of us took two children each, we could probably tend them very well until Francelia is able to get back to the meadow." This seemed a reasonable suggestion and everybody decided it should be acted upon. A family of mice agreed to take Reginald and Rose. Some bluebirds volunteered to look after Launcelot and Violet. A chipmunk family said they would provide for Cedric and Tulip. At this point a great bullfrog cleared his throat importantly.

"*Harrumph, harrumph,*" he began. "I notice that each of you is offering to take care of one boy and one girl. Now we frogs and toads, *harrumph*, want to do our share, but I don't think a dainty little girl would be happy living with us. I propose that we take the rest of the boys if others will look after the girls. *Harrumph.*"

The wisdom of the bullfrog's judgment was undeniable. It was decided that Christopher and Sebastian would be the responsibility of the bullfrogs. Algernon and Chauncey would be cared for by the toads, who promised to furnish them mouse food and not toad food. A swallow family offered to take Daisy and Pansy, and some meadowlarks said they would care for Lily and Iris.

Then a new problem occurred to Francelia's friends. Some of the little mice could simply go to live with the creatures that had offered to care for them. Mice and chipmunks, for example, could provide very comfortable living quarters. But songbirds and frogs, though they could feed and care for little mice well enough, couldn't furnish a safe place to sleep at night, nor could the toads be depended upon to come up with anything very satisfactory. A garter snake proposed the solution.

"Let them stay in Francelia's nest. We garter snakes will guard them, and they will be as safe as if their mother were at home." Garter snakes, though actually splendid, friendly little creatures, are not especially liked by others who do not know them well. If there were several snakes slithering around the vicinity of Francelia's nest, unwelcome visitors could be trusted to stay away.

Finally the creatures of Sweetgrass Meadow seemed to have things worked out for Francelia's children. They made much of the importance of keeping up games and dancing each pleasant day so that all the brothers and sisters would be able to play together, and resolved to keep their ears open for news of Francelia, who they were sure would return to her family as soon as she could.

Chapter Eight

In spite of everyone's efforts to care for Francelia's children and keep their spirits up, the days that followed were difficult. All the little mice missed their mother, especially the girls, and meadow activities weren't as much fun. The children had much kind attention and plenty to eat, but it became clear that something new and different would have to be devised to keep them cheerful in their mother's absence. Then something happened that gave not only Francelia's fourteen but all the other children — and even some of the younger adults — a new and interesting pastime when their bellies were full and the hawks were not about.

One afternoon another group of people came for a picnic in the meadow. This time there was no long, expensive-looking automobile, but three vehicles that looked like big boxes on wheels. They were brightly colored with pictures painted on their sides, and when they stopped and their doors were opened, loud, cheerful music came from within. The people in these strange large boxes were a bit unusual too. They were not children, but neither did they seem to be adults, exactly. They all wore the same kind of sturdy-looking, faded blue pants and shirts with pictures or words on them. They laughed a lot and ran about with the enthusiasm of children. They played musical instruments while others sang, and instead of sitting down to a formal picnic on a fine white cloth, they ate and drank the good things they had brought when and where they pleased.

The meadow creatures who gathered to watch found

these visitors so fascinating that they practically forgot about the tasty crumbs that would be lying about after the picnic had ended. The people, however, seemed in no hurry to leave.

After everybody had eaten, something was said about getting the pigskin out of the van. A young man ran to one of the big boxes. When he returned, he brought the strangest object the meadow creatures had ever seen.

The young man appeared at first to have a huge nut. It was partly round and partly longish, which is the right shape for a nut, and it was brown, which is the right color for a nut. But when the young man kicked it, it bounced off his foot and sailed high into the air. No meadow creature had ever seen a nut do that. Soon everybody at the picnic was kicking the object, throwing it or catching it.

After a while the people began to play a game of some sort. They divided into two teams that took turns moving the object toward opposite ends of the meadow. Sometimes a team ran with the object and sometimes they threw it. When a person carrying the object was touched by a member of the opposite team, everything stopped for a moment and then began again. There was a lot of good-natured pushing and shoving and chasing and even a bit of falling down and rolling around. When one of the teams managed to take the strange object all the way to the end of the meadow, there was much cheering and laughter. The game looked like great fun to the meadow creatures.

"I believe the object must be a ball of some sort," said an especially athletic chipmunk.

"I wonder whether we could learn to play that game," said Algernon. It was clear that not only he but all of Francelia's little boys, together with the boy toads and frogs and chipmunks and garter snakes and mice from other families wanted to play this game themselves. The little girls were not quite so taken with what they saw, but even they seemed to like it well enough, at least the part that had to do with chasing one another and bumping into one another.

"If that is a ball, where would we ever get one small enough for us to use?" asked Launcelot.

"What about a nut?" asked Chauncey.

"Too hard," answered a toad. "We couldn't kick it."

"Wait a minute," said a bluebird. "I think I can help. If I brought you a butternut down from a tree it would still be green and spongy. I bet that would work."

Everybody thought this was a good suggestion. The meadow creatures began to study the ball game carefully so that they would know how to play it when the people went away.

The next morning the bluebird delivered a fresh, green, spongy butternut to the meadow as she had promised. Everybody quickly formed into teams so that play could begin. It was decided that Francelia's children, who were beginning to grow big and strong, should play together as one team so that they could have the experience of working together as a family.

They first opposed a team of nearly grown mice and chipmunks, who proved too skillful for them, but they fared better in a second game against the frogs and toads. Nobody really worried too much about the score or who won or lost. They simply had a jolly time playing this new game, which they gradually realized was what people call football. As everyone learned more about playing it, the contests became even more fun, and within a few days a league was formed comprised of three teams of mice, three of chipmunks, two of toads, and two of frogs. The garter snakes and songbirds, finding themselves not very well suited to playing, were simply content to be spectators.

The meadow creatures named their league The Sweetgrass Meadow Touch Football Association. The teams would play games four days a week until the end of October. After that, the season would end because the butternuts would be too dry to make good footballs. On the last day of October there would be a final game between the two best teams, followed by a Halloween party in the afternoon before dark, when the owls began their hunting.

Francelia's children took part in these contests with eagerly, but they couldn't be expected to keep up with their friends who were practically grown and much stronger. Besides, they couldn't practice as much as some of the teams because they had to spend part of each morning learning to gather food and live safely in the meadow. One surprising development was that three of Francelia's little girls became excellent backfield players, probably because they had a natural talent for scurrying around. At the end of the season Francelia's children were in fifth place and watched the final, championship game, called the Butternut Bowl, from the sidelines.

Halloween day turned out to be perfect for a football game and a party. The sky was very bright and clear and the air was cool without being nippy. Not surprisingly, the championship contest in the Butternut Bowl was between the strongest teams of mice and chipmunks. The Whitefoot children's team cheered for the mice, but were disappointed when the chipmunks proved the winners. The chipmunks had the advantage of carrying a butternut in their cheek pouches, which permitted them to run faster when they had the ball. The mice gave a good account of themselves, however, and when the game ended everyone agreed that the addition of football to the activities in Sweetgrass Meadow had made it a most exciting October.

The Halloween party was a splendid affair. There was a quantity of fruit and nuts; someone even brought a bit of maple sugar. After a singing contest, a frog suggested country dances, which also proved a great success.

As dusk approached and the last dance was ending, a swallow flew into the meadow with simply astonishing news. He had been talking with a swallow who knew other birds from a colony quite a distance away. The swallows in that colony were well acquainted with Francelia, who was safe and healthy but forced by a series of accidents to remain where she was for the moment. The swallow reported that Francelia was worried about her children and missed them terribly, but couldn't say exactly when she would return to the meadow. She would come home just as soon as it was possible for her to do so.

Chapter Nine

News of Francelia came so late in the evening that there was no chance for discussion until the following day. NOTHING is more important than that the small creatures of the meadow be home by dusk. No one slept very soundly that night for thinking of the strange and wonderful news that the swallow had brought. No one could figure out how Francelia had wandered so far from Sweetgrass Meadow nor why her return was delayed.

"I don't suppose we'll really understand what happened until Francelia is able to return and tell us herself," said the mother mouse in the family looking after Reginald and Rose. "Right now I think we should do everything we can to help her children learn to care for themselves. Francelia may not get back to us for weeks yet."

"Very true," said a bullfrog who was caring for Christopher and Sebastian. "The time will soon come when we frogs will need to burrow into the mud for the winter season. The songbirds have already delayed their migration to a warmer climate so that they can continue to help."

Everybody quickly realized that a new problem was indeed developing. Although winters in Sweetgrass Meadow were rather mild with only an occasional snow, many of the friends who were caring for Francelia's children would soon need to change their manner of living. The frogs and toads would find soft places in the mud at the edge of the pond to rest for the winter months. The chipmunks would go into their dens to sleep through the harshest weather, and most of the songbirds would move to a warmer place to live until spring returned. The mice who remained active in the meadow could hardly be expected to care for all of the children when food was less plentiful and they had to work hard just to provide for themselves.

A meeting of all the creatures caring for the young mice was called immediately. Within an hour they had gathered in a sunny, sheltered corner of the meadow. Since everybody was already aware of the problem, there was no need to discuss it but only to find a practical solution to safeguard the well-being of Francelia's children.

Matters were quickly taken in hand by the wise old mouse who many weeks before had guessed that Francelia was about to have her babies.

"I have brought up many children myself," she said, "and I have never seen a brighter, more capable bunch than the fourteen we have to deal with. Now the time when we all can remain in the meadow and help these youngsters is admittedly growing short, but if we make a special effort for two or three more weeks to train them, showing them the dangers to be avoided and the skills to be improved, they will no doubt be able to get through the winter very nicely on their own. The weather has been good this year and there are lots of seeds and nuts lying about. There are still a few good apples in the orchard, and a piece of cheese still arrives from the barn once in a while. I don't think the children will have too much trouble getting enough to eat."

"As for lodgings, Francelia's nest is in good shape," she went on, "but is now too small to hold fourteen half-grown mice. If we repaired the old chipmunk den on the other side of the great oak tree and put that to use, however, we could be certain that all of the children would have a warm and secure shelter."

When the wise old mouse had finished speaking, everybody agreed that what she had said made good sense and seemed the best way to provide for Francelia's children. There didn't seem to be any other reasonable solution to their difficulties. The fourteen young mice were then called to the gathering and matters were explained to them. Being a brave, sensible family, they were quite matter-of-fact about the news that they would soon have to look after themselves.

"We understand how things are and can only be grateful for all you have done for us," said Cedric, acting as spokesman for the group. "I think we had better begin our training to be self-sufficient as soon as this meeting ends."

Before the day was over nearly all of the meadow creatures were busy with the tasks that would occupy them in the weeks that followed. Soft grasses were again added to Francelia's nest, and stout twigs fixed about the outside walls to make them strong for the months ahead. The chipmunk den was enlarged, repaired and then lined with the same soft grasses used in the other nest. A large quantity of seeds and nuts and bits of dried apple were stored among the roots of the great oak tree.

While all of this was going on, the young mice were trained to look after themselves once they were on their own. Adult mice took the lead in training Francelia's youngsters, but there was also special instruction from the frogs about the pond and from the chipmunks, who were excellent builders, about keeping the den in good repair. The songbirds, especially knowledgeable about the airy spaces above the meadow, helped teach the mice how to look out for hawks and avoid them. Everybody offered advice about staying strictly within doors after the sun had gone down.

By the middle of November everyone felt that Francelia's children would soon be able to fend for themselves. It became clear that time was growing very short when the garter snakes came to bid Francelia's children goodbye one morning. They could no longer delay crawling beneath a large pile of rocks at the edge of the meadow to sleep through the winter months.

The parting was not a very happy occasion. One young fellow had become such good friends with Iris that he regretted a little that he had not been born a mouse or Iris a garter snake. There were promises not to forget good friendships through the winter months and vows of a grand reunion and jolly game of tag on the first warm day of spring.

After the garter snakes had departed, several of the older

folks remained in a little group to discuss the tearful parting that they had just witnessed.

"It's going to be awfully hard on Francelia's children to say goodbye to us a few at a time," said a particularly warmhearted toad. "I feel sure that they will get along all right through the winter months. I don't really worry about that at all any more. But I am disturbed to think that they will have to go through these sad little farewells nearly every day now until we are all gone until spring."

"I know," said a meadowlark. "It would be a lot better if we could end the year in a happy way, with everyone saying goodbye to one another together."

"I have an idea," said a chipmunk. "Why don't we plan a great feast for sometime toward the end of this week? We can have some games and then a big, hearty meal. That way we will be reminded of all the pleasures of living among friends in a beautiful place like Sweetgrass Meadow. It will be easier for all of us if we say goodbye for the winter in a happy mood. After all, we ALL have a lot to be thankful for."

The chipmunk's suggestion proved just the thing to get everybody back into a cheerful frame of mind. It was quickly agreed that at the end of the week a final day of games and good food would be arranged, and the meadow creatures set about preparations for the feast to which everyone could now look forward.

Chapter Ten

When the inhabitants of the meadow awoke on the morning of the great feast, they found that a light frost had settled during the night. The sky was cloudless, however, and though the season was late, the sun quickly warmed the air. The day promised to be beautiful, more pleasant than most that would pass before next spring.

"I'm glad we have only a light frost to think about," grumbled a bullfrog. "It's late enough for a hard freeze to come any time now, and I want to be comfortably settled in the mud before that happens."

"I've already got my winter spot picked out," observed another frog. "The softest, gooiest, blackest patch of mud that ever comforted the heart of a bullfrog. When the feast ends today I'm going to light out for my patch by the pond just as quickly as I can. I get plain excited thinking of how good it will feel to wallow down in that thick, black slime and get settled for a long winter's nap. It just makes me tingle all over." A chipmunk who happened to be listening managed to hide the little shudder that ran through him and said only that he too had prepared his winter spot, a comfortable den beneath an old log, and that he too expected to go in for the winter at the end of the day.

Before mid-morning the frost had disappeared and the meadow seemed as warm as it had been in September. Everyone entered into the games and dancing as light-heartedly as they had in summer. When the toad who was vain of his dancing proposed a contest, it was quickly begun. As a kind of going-away present from his friends, he was allowed to win the contest, though in truth he didn't dance a bit better than he had many weeks before when he and his associates had been vanquished by Francelia's children. A chorus of bluebirds and swallows gave a little recital just before noon, and then there was a vigorous game of tag, which so whetted everyone's appetite that there were calls for the feast to begin. Now feasts don't ordinarily begin before mid afternoon, but since everyone was hungry and wanted plenty of time to say their goodbyes before the early November dusk fell, the food was put out and the dining began.

A banquet table had been made from an old board lying in the meadow, and the resourcefulness of the food committee amazed everyone who now saw the mountain of good things heaped upon it. There were sunflower seeds and Sweetgrass seeds and cracked corn, walnuts and butternuts and hickory nuts. Somehow a great piece of cheese had been obtained, as well as apples and a few pears. Someone had mixed some pumpkin with honey and spices for a large pumpkin pudding. Several pieces of maple sugar were on the table, and even several large cookies. The inhabitants of Sweetgrass Meadow declared that there had never before been such a feast, and they ate until they were virtually stuffed.

Earlier in the week, when the grand affair was being planned, someone had suggested an after-dinner speech. A clever old mouse who was known for his large assortment of

amusing stories had agreed to entertain his friends and neighbors with a few appropriate remarks. As the meal concluded, he rose and moved toward one end of the banquet table to begin his speech. Being a rather theatrical mouse, he made as much of striding to the spot he had chosen and rising onto his hind legs as he could. But when he finally began to speak he found he had the attention of no one.

At the other end of the table was a path toward the dairy barn. Everyone who a moment before had been gathered around the table was moving toward the path, making it impossible to see very well what was causing all the excitement. Something was moving down the path — that much was clear. A sharp-eyed meadowlark flew up from the ground for a better look.

"It's Francelia," he sang out to the gathering below, "and she has somebody with her."

At this announcement there was a great rush down the path. Francelia's children led the throng, followed by the other mice and chipmunks, frogs, and toads. The songbirds flew into the air to greet Francelia, but they didn't fly too fast, because they knew it was only right for Francelia's children to reach her first.

The reunion that followed was the most exciting thing that anyone in the meadow could remember. At first there was tremendous confusion — hugging, kissing, laughing, crying, squeaking, twittering, croaking, and more squeaking. Everyone tried to talk at once, eager to understand where Francelia had been, her adventures, and how she had finally managed to return home. Everyone could see that she was in good health but a little worn from what had obviously been a long journey to return to Sweetgrass Meadow. Her companion was a lean, strong, handsome, quiet-spoken mouse named Adam, who seemed most protective of Francelia.

"You must be starved from your journey," a sensible chipmunk finally thought to say. "We have just had dinner and there is lots of food left over. Come and get something to eat and then perhaps we'll all be calm enough to ask questions one at a time and listen to the story I'm sure you have to tell us."

With her children crowded around her, Francelia moved to the banquet table to eat. The best of the remaining food was placed before her and Adam. In spite of the perfect table manners natural to Francelia and also, it seemed, to Adam, everyone could see that they were very hungry and waited quietly until they had eaten their fill. Even Francelia's children, much as they wanted to hover close to their mother, didn't crowd their mother as she ate to restore her strength. When she had eaten all she wanted, Francelia gathered her children to her and looked around at her friends.

"What perfect care you have taken of my children while I was gone," she said. "I felt all the time I was away from the meadow that my friends would somehow provide for my little ones, but I never expected to see them so strong and healthy and well-cared for as they appear today. I'll never be able to thank you enough, but I shall do my best all the same.

"You probably wonder how a mother could wander off and leave her babies in the first place," Francelia continued. "I hope you know that I would never have allowed myself to become separated from my little children if I could have helped it. But as you all realize, unfortunate accidents sometimes can't be helped. I'll try to tell you my story, but I must warn you that it is long and complicated and I'll have to leave some details out if we are all to be safely home by dusk." And here is the story that Francelia told:

Chapter Eleven

"The evening before I disappeared was a very hard one for me. I had worked all that day to provide enough food for my children, and though I had help from friends who had more food than they needed, I could see that some of my little boys, who were beginning to be very active as boys are, were going to bed hungry. There is NOTHING more difficult for a mother than to see her little ones unhappy because they have not had enough to eat. At least that is my opinion. I decided to risk a couple of more trips into the meadow for food even though the sky was nearly dark and the owls would soon be out.

"At the edge of the meadow closest to the dairy barn was a large patch of sunflower plants that the farmers had grown, I suppose to get seeds for the birds that they feed in their yard during the winter months. I knew there would be lots of seeds on the ground near those plants, and I went there as quickly as I could to gather food. It took me several trips to carry all the seeds I needed back to my nest, but I finally saw that by making one last visit to the sunflower patch, I could put all my children to bed with full bellies.

"When I left my nest that last time it was completely dark. I reached the sunflower patch without trouble, but just as I began to pick up a last few seeds I heard a horribly frightening cry very close to me. An owl was hunting directly above the sunflower patch! I managed to hide in a clump of grass nearby, but I rustled some dry grass in doing so. I was sure that the owl had heard me because he remained very close and continued to cry out, hoping to scare me into moving so that he could seize me and carry me away. I was terribly afraid, for I knew that sooner or later I would be found. There seemed to be no way to escape the cruel owl, who was drawing closer every minute.

"Then an idea came to me, one that I felt would save me even if it created new difficulties later on. At the edge of the clump of grass where I was hidden was a small stream that flows away from the meadow, through the yard of the farmhouse beside the dairy barn. I knew that the owl would never think to look for a mouse in the water, and I saw that there was a piece of bark at the water's edge that was just big enough for me to float on. Very carefully I moved from my hiding place to the piece of bark. I pushed it into the water and climbed on top of it, barely wetting my feet.

For the moment I was safe.

"I had been in such terrible danger from the owl that I really didn't think much about where the stream would flow to or how I would get out of the water and back to my nest in the meadow. I now realized that the stream moved much more quickly than I had thought and that there was nothing to do but remain on my piece of bark and hope for the best. I floated through the yard past the farmhouse, which looked warm and cheerful and made me lonely for my own comfortable home and precious children. After the stream left the yard, it flowed through a huge metal pipe beneath

the road in front of the farmhouse. When it came out on the other side of the road, it almost immediately joined a much larger stream, from which I saw that I would not be able to escape until my piece of bark finally came to rest against the bank.

"For the remainder of the night I floated farther and farther away from my home and children in Sweetgrass Meadow. The stream — it was actually a small river — flowed beside the road for some distance and then finally turned away into an immense cornfield. The river now moved more slowly than before, but I thought it best not to leave my piece of bark and try to swim to shore. The moon had risen and I could see that both banks of the river were lined with great stalks of corn where I would find little shelter and no new friends to help me in my terrible predicament.

"Just after daybreak the cornfield ended. On one bank of the river was a large farm with several buildings where I felt sure some friendly mice would be living. I decided that I had better leave my piece of bark and try to swim to shore, for I felt I had a better chance of finding safety in one of the farm buildings than would come my way again. I am not a very good swimmer, but I found the strength to reach the bank of the river and once more put my feet on solid ground. I was very tired, yet I knew I wouldn't be safe until I reached shelter. I ran to the closest farm building as quickly as I could and crawled through a small hole into a space in the wall. I looked about for a moment to be sure I hadn't stumbled into some new danger and then, when I was satisfied that I could rest for at least a little while, I curled up in a corner and went to sleep.

"When I awoke about midday, I was not alone. I had been found by a mouse named Archie, who was both the bravest and most reckless mouse I have ever met. He even stood up to the much larger rats at the farm who often times acted like bullies. He wasn't awfully polite and he chewed tobacco and showed off a lot, but he was very kind to me at the first when I was lonely and frightened. Anyway, Archie showed me how to get to the loft of the building where I had found shelter. The loft was safe from the several cats that were about the farmyard, and it was half full of sacks of old corn which was very good to eat.

"There was a large window in the loft which let in lots of light and made it a warm, bright, pleasant place. Archie introduced me to many new friends and helped me get settled. Everyone pointed out to me that in spite of my great fear for my children I would have to stay where I was for the moment. In the first place I was still tired and worn from my ordeal on the river. Then I had only the faintest idea of how to get back to Sweetgrass Meadow and needed time to find my bearings before setting out. But the biggest reason for delay was that the cornfield would soon be harvested, and to be caught in the cornfield when men began to move through it with their enormous machines meant certain destruction. For all of these reasons I had to trust that my friends would look after my children until it was safer for me to return home.

"My life in the farm building was not unhappy. I made new friends who were kind and helpful and seemed to understand how hard it was for me to be so far from my home and family. I also lost my friend Archie. One night he went down from the loft for some tobacco in a pouch a farmer had left on a windowsill. We all warned him of the danger in going downstairs at night, but he just laughed and said that he wasn't scared and that no cat in the world could keep him from a good chew of tobacco. We never saw Archie again.

"One morning we heard a great deal of noise in the farmyard. Looking out the window in the loft, we saw that the farmers were taking machines into the field to harvest their corn. I knew that I could soon begin to plan for my long journey home. By now I had a pretty clear idea of what direction to travel to reach Sweetgrass Meadow, and though I knew the journey would be dangerous, I felt I could probably make it successfully. It was about then that Adam, whom I saw every day in the loft but who had always been very quiet, declared his admiration for me and his willingness to travel with me and help me reach my destination. Adam also pointed out a difficulty that I hadn't considered, namely, that my home was not only far away

but on the other side of the river, which we would have to find some means of crossing. I accepted Adam's offer of help, and he has been my loyal companion to this day.

"The farmers were busy in the field for nearly a week. I spent the time eating and resting so that I would be fit and strong when I began my journey. Adam and I also planned as best we could what route we would take and how we would guard against the dangers we would almost certainly encounter. One afternoon we heard the farmers bring their machines back to the farmyard and put them away in a large building. That was about two weeks ago. We decided to begin our journey the next day if the weather was fair.

"When we awoke in the morning the sun was up. Adam and I said goodbye to our friends quickly because we knew our first day would be very long and tiring. We were going to cut straight across the immense field where the corn had been standing to reach the river. There seemed to be little danger from hawks in the field, and we felt that by running across that great open space we would make our journey days shorter. Our plan worked, but when we reached the river about nightfall I was so tired that we had to find shelter in the roots of a tree and recover for a day or two.

"About the time I felt strong enough to resume our journey a rainy spell set in. This delayed us, but it allowed me further rest before we set off upriver. During all this time Adam left our shelter every day and gathered enough

71

food for us both to eat. Finally, about a week ago, we started along the riverbank in the direction of home. In just a day or two we were opposite the dairy farm that stands in front of Sweetgrass Meadow, but we had to continue upriver until we found a place to cross. We now moved very slowly because we were constantly looking for an opportunity of some kind that would allow us to move to the other bank of the river. The day before yesterday we came to a wooden bridge that farmers use to drive their trucks and machines across the river. We crossed the bridge and found a safe place to spend the night.

"Yesterday we had our strangest adventure of all. We were traveling along the edge of the road that runs beside the river and passes in front of the dairy farm. About mid-morning we noticed a funny little red, white, and blue car far behind us coming down the road very slowly. It stopped in front of every farm it came to, and a man in the car put pieces of paper into little boxes on posts by the roadside. Adam and I waited beside one of these boxes on a post, and when the car arrived at it, we hopped up on a sort of little shelf at the back of the car. By early afternoon yesterday we had ridden practically home. Because a large dog was prowling about the farmyard, we found shelter and waited for a good chance this morning to come into the meadow. That chance didn't occur until this afternoon. I was terribly anxious to see you all, and we were both very hungry because we hadn't eaten in two days, but Adam showed me that, having arrived so close to home, it was still necessary to be patient and not take any foolish risks. We finally were able to leave our hiding place this afternoon.

It took us just a little while to come through the farmyard and into the meadow that I love so dearly. I hope I shall never have to leave it again."

When Francelia had finished her story, both her children and the other meadow creatures agreed that it was a truly wonderful tale, especially because it ended happily with the reunion that had made their festive day complete. It was now late afternoon, and everybody turned to the matter of saying goodbye to friends for the winter. The frogs and toads were the first to leave the party, hopping away to their lovely patches of black mud at the edge of the pond in Sweetgrass Meadow. The chipmunks were safely curled up in their dens by the time that dusk fell, and the songbirds flew up into trees from which they would leave at the first light of dawn to fly to the warm places where they would spend the winter.

Francelia, her children, and the other meadow mice all got home safely and continued to see one another on the more pleasant days in the months that followed. But there was no really large or complete gathering of meadow creatures from that day until the following spring, and everyone always remembered that year as having ended with the great feast and Francelia's return to her family and friends.

Chapter Twelve

What happened to Francelia and her children and friends the next year is really another story, but it should be reported that everyone came through the winter safely. There was another grand reunion and celebration in the meadow when warm weather returned in the spring. Shortly after that Francelia and Adam had a family of baby mice — only five this time, three boys and two little girls.

By spring Francelia's first family were all nearly adults and beginning to think of mates and nests and families themselves. They grew up to be a truly splendid assortment of mice, though a bit unusual. Reginald, who is the most like his father, is a great talker and rather vain of his magnificent white head and neck. He talks from time to time about how nice it would be if all of the mice were to choose themselves a king and points out that to be king a mouse would need to be very handsome and have a distinctive coat of fur, perhaps with a light-colored hood covering the head and maybe even the neck. His sister Rose, who is truly beautiful in a dark hood of fur above her white body, is sweet and modest like her mother and would never think of being queen.

The fairly long period when Francelia's children were cared for not by mice but by other creatures in the meadow has had an interesting effect, too. Cedric and Tulip, who were raised by chipmunks, though they are very handsome creatures, appear to have had their brown and white spots rearranged so that if one looks at them from just the right angle, they seem to have stripes running down their backs. They are also pouchy about the cheeks and quite as happy to sleep in a den at night as in a nest of soft grasses.

The foster-children of the bluebirds, Violet and Launcelot, whose coats were originally silver-tan in color, now have a rich bluish cast to their fur. Daisy and Pansy have developed a very peculiar squeak which sounds much like the twittering of swallows to anyone who listens carefully.

Christopher and Sebastian are excellent swimmers, and both they and Algernon and Chauncey seem to hop more than scurry as they move about the meadow playing games or looking for a bite to eat. All four of these young fellows are very fond of mud and have to be reminded from time to time that a gentlemanly young mouse always keeps his fur clean and neatly groomed.

All of the mice who were protected by garter snakes while they slept in the nest beneath the great oak tree have the ability to slither, which they demonstrate on occasion. This talent is especially amusing in Christopher, Sebastian, Algernon and Chauncey, who are the only creatures in Sweetgrass Meadow or any other meadow who can hop and slither at the same time.

But for all their peculiarities, Francelia's fourteen children have grown up to be good citizens of the meadow, devoted to their mother, respectful to Adam, and kind to their little half-brothers and sisters, whom they will soon begin to teach such games as tag and hide-and-seek. No one who knows them can doubt that in spite of the difficulties they had to face when they were but children, they are now a credit to all who helped bring them up and a source of great pride for their admiring mother.